A Robbie Reader

ADAM & LEVINE

John Bankston

Mitchell Lane
PUBLISHERS
P.O. Box 196
Hockessin, Delaware 19707
Visit us on the web: www.mitchelllane.com

Mitchell Lane
PUBLISHERS

Printing   1   2   3   4   5   6   7   8   9

A Robbie Reader Biography

Abigail Breslin
Adam Levine
Adrian Peterson
Albert Einstein
Albert Pujols
Aly and AJ
Andrew Luck
AnnaSophia Robb
Ariana Grande
Ashley Tisdale
Brenda Song
Brittany Murphy
Bruno Mars
Buster Posey
Charles Schulz
Chris Johnson
Cliff Lee
Dale Earnhardt Jr.
Darius Rucker
David Archuleta
Demi Lovato

Derrick Rose
Donovan McNabb
Drake Bell & Josh Peck
Dr. Seuss
Dwayne "The Rock" Johnson
Dwyane Wade
Dylan & Cole Sprouse
Emily Osment
Hilary Duff
Jamie Lynn Spears
Jennette McCurdy
Jesse McCartney
Jimmie Johnson
Joe Flacco
Jonas Brothers
Keke Palmer
Larry Fitzgerald
LeBron James
Mia Hamm

Miguel Cabrera
Miley Cyrus
Miranda Cosgrove
Philo Farnsworth
Raven-Symoné
Rixton
Robert Griffin III
Roy Halladay
Shaquille O'Neal
Story of Harley-Davidson
Sue Bird
Syd Hoff
Tiki Barber
Tim Howard
Tim Lincecum
Tom Brady
Tony Hawk
Troy Polamalu
Victor Cruz
Victoria Justice

Library of Congress Cataloging-in-Publication Data
Bankston, John, 1974–
   Adam Levine / by John Bankston.
      pages cm. — (Robbie reader)
   Includes bibliographical references and index.
   ISBN 978-1-68020-096-6 (library bound)
   1. Levine, Adam, 1979– —Juvenile literature. 2. Rock musicians—United States—Biography—Juvenile literature. I. Title.
   ML3930.L38B36 2015
   782.42166092—dc23
   [B]
                                                      2015003208
eBook ISBN: 978-1-68020-097-3

ABOUT THE AUTHOR: Born in Boston, Massachusetts, John Bankston began writing articles while still a teenager. Since then, over two hundred of his articles have been published in magazines and newspapers across the country, including travel articles in *The Tallahassee Democrat, The Orlando Sentinel,* and *The Tallahassean.* He is the author of over sixty biographies for young adults, including works on Alicia Keys, Missy Elliot, Eminem, scientist Stephen Hawking, author F. Scott Fitzgerald and actor Jodi Foster. He loves popular music. Besides Maroon 5, he enjoys Selena Gomez, Skrillex, Pretty Reckless and Iggy Azalea.

PUBLISHER'S NOTE: The following story has been thoroughly researched and to the best of our knowledge represents a true story. While every possible effort has been made to ensure accuracy, the publisher will not assume liability for damages caused by inaccuracies in the data, and makes no warranty on the accuracy of the information contained herein. This story has not been authorized or endorsed by Adam Levine.

TABLE OF CONTENTS

Words in bold type can be found in the glossary.

Adam Levine often plays his music on talk shows. Here he laughs during an appearance on Late Night With Jimmy Fallon *on June 14, 2013.*

A Dream Come True

Every February, musicians gather for the Grammy Awards. There are awards for Record of the Year, Album of the Year, and Song of the Year. Over eighty Grammy Awards are handed out. Usually the one for Best New Artist gets the most attention.

Over the past 55 years, many Best New Artist winners became **famous**. In 2014, Macklemore and Ryan Lewis won the award. Past winners include Carrie Underwood, Christina Aguilera and Adele.

In 2005, Adam's band, Maroon 5, was **nominated** for two Grammy Awards. When they won for Best New Artist, Adam said, "It was genuinely shocking. I really didn't think it was going to happen."

Of his bandmates Adam said, "These are my best friends, and this is the trippiest thing I've ever gone through in my life."

Although Maroon 5 won Best New Artist, they were not a new band. Levine and most of the group began playing together in high school. Winning the Grammy was a dream come true. It was a dream Adam Levine first had as a boy, growing up in Brentwood, California.

Adam and Maroon 5 often play special events. Here they perform during the Neighborhood Inaugural Ball on January 20, 2009 honoring President Barack Obama.

Either as a presenter or as an award winner, Adam is a regular at the Grammy's. During the 54th Annual Grammy Awards on February 2, 2012, he paused to pose with current girlfriend, model Anne V.

Successful bands don't just play at arenas. They also play high paying corporate events. Here Adam and Maroon 5 keyboardist PJ Morton perform at the 2013 consumer electronics show in Las Vegas, Nevada.

Living in California

Although Brentwood is not as well known as Hollywood, the **neighborhood** where Adam Levine grew up is home to many of California's rich and famous. Hip-hop artist Dr. Dre, actor Jim Carrey, and actress Gwyneth Paltrow have all lived in Brentwood. Located on L.A.'s west side, the neighborhood of some 33,000 people lies between Westwood and Santa Monica.

Adam Noah Levine was born in Los Angeles, California on March 18, 1979. His mother, Patsy Noah, was an admissions counselor. His father Fred founded the successful retail chain M. Fredric. He has two brothers, Michael and Sam, and two stepsisters, Liza and Julia.

In 2013, Maroon 5 was nominated for two Grammy Awards. Band members James Valentine, Adam Levine, PJ Morton, Matt Flynn and Mickey Madden posed outside the Staples Center in Los Angeles before the awards.

When Adam was seven, his parents divorced. Afterward, he spent weekends with his father and he spent the rest of the week with his mom. It was hard. As an adult he described his blended family to *Details* magazine as, "Steps, halves—at least 30 minutes of explaining [the] family-tree . . . But I have a big, wonderful family."

Adam began taking guitar lessons when he was ten. Two years later, he performed for the first time at the Troubadour, a well-known Los Angeles nightclub. He was too nervous to face the audience.

Although Adam's father and grandmother were Jewish, when he turned thirteen he decided not to have a **bar mitzvah**—the religion's traditional coming of age ceremony. He didn't want to get money and gifts, telling *The Jewish Chronicle*, "I just don't think it's the most respectful way to deal with God and beliefs . . . "

Adam became friends with future movie stars Jonah Hill and Jason Segal. While attending Brentwood School, he met Jesse Carmichael, Ryan Dusick and Mickey Madden. They decided to form a band. Adam would be the band's lead singer, and play guitar alongside Mickey. Jesse would play keyboards and Ryan would be the drummer. They named the band Kara's Flowers, after a girl they had a crush on. Adam figured if the band did well, girls like Kara would notice him.

Maroon 5 was once an opening act. Now they are headliners. Here Adam sings in Virginia Beach, Virginia where he performed with Counting Crows and Sara Barellis.

No More Flowers

Adam Levine dreamed of being a rock star but wanted to disappear. "I was a mess," he admitted to *People* magazine. "I had really bad acne and hid under a hat . . . I had no confidence."

Adam's band Kara's Flowers practiced until they felt they could play in front of a crowd. Musicians call performing live a "gig." Kara's Flowers' first gig was at the Whiskey a Go-Go on Los Angeles's Sunset Strip. Famous bands like the Doors, Janis Joplin and Led Zeppelin have played there.

Kara's Flowers performed in clubs and private parties across Los Angeles. Adam also worked part-time for his father at the M. Fredric Warehouse. "As soon as [Adam's]

Playing on a radio station show can help a band get discovered. In 2003, Maroon 5 was not well known when Adam sang at 97.3 Alice's Now and Zen Festival in San Francisco on September 21, 2003.

Dad would leave the office," an employee recalled on the company's website, "Adam would pull out his guitar and play for the warehouse staff; which they loved because he was way too slow of a worker!"

When Adam was sixteen, Kara's Flowers played in the beach town of Malibu where a recording label scout heard them. The scout's job was to discover new talent for Reprise Records. In 1997, the band signed a record deal. They worked with producer Rob Cavallo, who had worked with the band Green Day. They appeared on the original *Beverly Hills 90210*. Adam thought he would soon be a star.

Instead, when Kara's Flower's first and only album was released in 1997, few people bought it. Reprise Records fired them. At eighteen, Adam Levine lost the only job he had ever wanted.

Adam isn't afraid to change his look. Here he sports a crewcut, print shirt and pink guitar for a May 6, 2015 appearance on Jimmy Kimmel Live.

Jane's Songs

Adam Levine traveled nearly three thousand miles to attend college and to pursue his dreams. Five Towns College trained students for careers in the music business. Located near New York City, the Dix Hills School didn't just teach Adam about the business; it taught him about the music.

Adam began enjoying different music styles like Rhythm and Blues and hip-hop. Bandmate and fellow Five Towns College student, Jesse Carmichael listened to jazz. They decided to form a new band with a different sound.

Attending school changed Adam's music. A woman changed his **lyrics**. "It was

17

the first time I was ever dumped," he told *People* magazine. Lying in bed with the covers over his head, he wrote: "If I could bottle up the chills that you give me, I would keep them in a jar next to my bed." He told *People*, "That was the best line I ever wrote in my life."

Despite the risk, Adam and Jesse dropped out of school. Returning to Los Angeles they joined up with Mickey Madden and Ryan Dussick. Jesse would now play piano, so they added a new guitarist, James Valentine. The band would now be called Maroon 5.

Their new sound wasn't popular. Audiences in Los Angeles wanted them to sound like other edgy rock bands. Levine told *Details*, "I wanted to sound like Michael Jackson and write pop songs."

Old connections and a new sound still helped them land a record deal. Their first album would be called *Songs about Jane*, about the woman who broke up with Adam.

Album sales determine where a band or singer "charts" (a recording chart that shows who is on top of the list with the best record sales). When Taylor Swift's album 1989 was released in October 28, 2014 it sold over one million copies its first week. It was the number one album in the U.S. When *Songs About Jane* was released in June of 2002, it sold less than two thousand copies. Maroon 5 looked like it would follow Kara's Flowers into failure and breakup.

The Z100 Jingle Ball is one of the biggest radio shows of the year. Adam and Maroon 5 were famous across the world when Adam performed during the 2014 show at New York's Madison Square Garden.

Today Adam does many different things, but continues to tour with Maroon 5. He returned to Madison Square Garden in 2015 as part of the band's "V" tour.

V

Maroon 5's first album was failing. Adam Levine had been fired by one record label. He didn't want to be fired by another.

Summer brought opportunity. Well-known bands and singers performed in concert halls and stadiums. Lesser-known bands went first, "opening" for them. Guitarist James Valentine knew John Mayer from music school. Over the summer of 2002, Mayer invited Maroon 5 to open.

Levine joked to *The Boston Herald* that, "Maroon 5 never sleeps." The hard work paid off. People came to see John Mayer and other headliners. They left talking about Maroon 5. They became fans, buying the band's album—and telling their friends.

Maroon 5's first album was selling better than ever two years after its release and by December 2004 it had sold three million. In the spring of 2004, "This Love" became a number one hit. "It's really unbelievable," Levine told the *Herald*. "This is just unheard of . . . "

In 2005, Maroon 5 won Best New Artist. *Songs About Jane* sold four million copies in the US. The band worried about their second album suffering a "**sophomore** slump." Bands often break-up or are fired by their recording label when a second album does poorly. Already Maroon 5 had hard choices. That year, Gavin DeGraw's drummer Matt Flynn replaced Ryan Dusick who had wrist problems.

In 2007, Maroon 5's second album of new songs, *It Won't Be Soon Before Long* sold millions of copies. A few years later, Adam took a new job.

In 2011, Adam Levine was asked to join NBC's musical **competition**, *The Voice*. Along with fellow coaches Christina Aguilera and Cee Lo Green, Adam would help singers become stars. "I'm not a great performer; I'm just uncomplicated," Adam admitted to *Men's Health*. He told **contestants** on *The Voice*, "The biggest thing is confidence—not false confidence but real confidence."

The Voice also helped Maroon 5's album *Hands All Over*. It didn't do well until the band added a new song with Christina Aguilera. "Moves Like Jagger" reached number one.

Adam Levine found a whole new career thanks to the NBC singing show, The Voice. Here he appears with co-hosts Blake Shelton, Christina Aguilera, Cee Lo Green and Carson Daly at a 2011 press conference for the show.

Adam Levine enjoyed single life, dating a number of well-known women. In 2014, he married model Behati Prinsloo. The couple paused for photos during closing night for New York's Tribeca Film Festival.

Confident and good-looking, Adam was a natural as an actor. He appeared in FX's *American Horror Story* and the movie *Can a Song Save Your Life?* with Keira Knightley.

Fans had read about the famous and pretty women Adam dated, including Jessica Simpson and Paris Hilton. On July 19, 2014 he married model Behati Prinsloo. The next month, Maroon 5 released their fifth album. It was titled with the Roman **numeral** for the number 5: *V*. The album would be nominated for three *Billboard* Music Awards. Maroon 5 was also nominated for a Nickelodeon Kids' Choice Award as Favorite Music Group.

Adam is one of the highest paid singers in the world, making around $35 million per year. Because of this, he is able to give quite a bit of

money to causes he believes in. Throughout his career, Adam has supported charities including the National Kidney Foundation, the Elton John AIDS Foundation and Shriners Hospitals for Children.

The band does their part by promoting charities on their webpage, including the work of Aid Still Required. The charity helps communities across the world recover from natural disasters.

Sometimes, it's Adam's music that means the most. Christopher Warner is a ten-year old boy with Down syndrome. His teacher made a video of Christopher singing some of the band's songs. After a local radio station arranged for Christopher to get backstage passes, Adam made a point of meeting the young fan. When Christopher grew shy, and stayed on the floor, Adam joined him and suggested others do so as well.

Adam continues to work making the music he loves. Always proud to be a role model, he plans to stay on the music scene for years to come.

As a popular and successful singer, Adam is able to promote causes he believes in. He does many different things, including performing during the keynote address at a 2013 consumer electronics show.

CHRONOLOGY

1979   Adam Noah Levine is born in Los Angeles, California.

1991   Performs live for the first time at Los Angeles club, The Troubadour.

1997   First band, Kara's Flowers, is signed to Reprise Records and released the album *The Fourth World*.

1998   Adam leaves California to attend Five Towns College in Dix, New York.

1999   After poor sales, Kara's Flowers is released from their recording contract by Reprise Records.

2002   New band Maroon 5 signs with Octone Records/J Records/BMG.

2002   Maroon 5 releases first album, *Songs About Jane*.

2004   Maroon 5 wins Grammy Award for Best New Artist.

2011   Adam Joins NBC singing competition for *The Voice* as a judge and coach.

2014   Levine marries model Behati Prinsloo in Cabos, Mexico.

2015   Produces *Songland*, a TV pilot featuring a songwriting competition for NBC.

2015   Maroon 5 kicks off their world tour in Dallas, Texas on February 16.

Discography

1997 *The Fourth World* (with Kara's Flowers)

2002 *Songs About Jane* (Maroon 5)

2004 1.22.03 Acoustic (Maroon 5)

2005 "Heard Em Say" (Single with Kanye West)

2005 *Live–Friday the Thirteenth* (Maroon 5)

2007 *It Won't Be Soon Before Long* (Maroon 5)

2010 *Hands All Over* (Maroon 5)

2011 "Stereo Hearts" (Single with Gym Class Heroes)

2012 "My Life" (Single with Eminem and 50 Cent)

2012 *Overexposed* (Maroon 5)

2014 *V* (Maroon 5)

FIND OUT MORE

Books

Tieck, Sarah. *Adam Levine (Big Buddy Biographies)*. Edina, MN: ABDO Publishing, 2013.

Rush, Teresa. *Adam Levine Quiz Book—50 Fun and Fact Filled Questions About Your Favorite Maroon 5 Star Adam Levine*. Kindle eBook, July 17, 2014.

On the Internet

Adam Levine—Billboard
http://www.billboard.com/artist/1481831/adam-levine

Maroon 5
http://www.maroon5.com/

The Voice
http://www.nbc.com/the-voice

Works Consulted

Newspapers

Katz, Larry. "Maroon Shot; Best New Band Heads for New Arena." *Boston Herald*, April 1, 2005.

Periodicals

Coulton, Antoinette, and Julie Jordan. "Adam Levine: Sexiest Man Alive." *People Weekly* 80, no. 23 (2013). http://www.people/archive/article/0,,20762896,00.html

Friend, Tad, "Electric Man," *The New Yorker*. July 21, 2014. http://www.newyorker.com/magazine/2014/07/21/electric-man

Lester, Paul. "Interview: Adam Levine," *The Jewish Chronicle Online*. February 11, 2011. http://www.thejc.com/arts/music/45058/interview-adam-levine

FIND OUT MORE

Jones, Finn-Olaf "Adam Levine's Hollywood Hills
    Home," *Architectural Digest*. March 2012.
    http://www.architecturaldigest.com/celebrity-
    homes/2012/adam-levine-hollywood-hills-home-article#

Marks, Craig. "Adam Levine: The New King of Pop," *Details*.
    June 1, 2012. http://www.details.com/culture-trends/
    cover-stars/201206/adam-levine-maroon-5-voice-
    interview?currentPage=

Websites

ABC News Maroon 5's Adam Levine's Playlist: Top 5 Songs
    That Impacted Rocker's Style
    http://abcnews.go.com/Entertainment/maroon-5s-
    adam-levines-playlist-top-songs-impacted/story?id=1496
    6693&singlePage=true

Adam Levine and Behati Prinsloo Are Married
    http://www.eonline.com/news/561010/adam-levine-
    and-behati-prinsloo-are-married

Annual Grammy Awards Nominees
    http://www.grammy.com/nominees

Best Song on Kanye West's *The College Dropout* Album
    http://www.rankopedia.com/Best-Song-on-Kanye-
    West's-'The-College-Dropout'-Album/Step1/14351/.htm

Billboard Maroon 5 Biography
    http://www.billboard.com/artist/309663/maroon-5/
    biography

Brentwood: Neighborhood Profile
    http://losangeles.about.com/od/neighborhoods/a/
    brentwood.htm

Glamour News-Adam Levine and Behati Prinsloo Pucker up
    for Kiss Cam. http://www.glamourmagazine.co.uk/news/
    celebrity/2013/07/17/adam-levine-engaged-behati-
    prinsloo-wedding-married-news

Rumor Confirmed: Dr. Dre Buys Tom and Gisele's Estate
http://www.zillow.com/blog/tom-and-gisele-estate-151584/
The 100 Best **Debut** Albums of All Time
http://www.rollingstone.com/music/lists/the-100-greatest-debut-albums-of-all-time-20130322/the-college-dropout-19691231
47th Annual GRAMMY Awards-Best New Artist
http://www.grammy.com/videos/47th-annual-grammy-awards-best-new-artist

GLOSSARY

bar mitzvah (bar-MITS-va)–Jewish religious ceremony held on a boy's thirteenth birthday.

competition (KOM-pi-tish-en)–activity done by group of people to see the one who is best.

contestant (kon-TES-tent)–person involved with a competition.

debut (day-BYOO)–First appearance.

famous–Well known.

lyrics (LEER-iks)–The words of a song.

neighborhood (NA-bor-HOOD)–A district or area.

nominate (NOM-in-ate)–To name as a possibility for an honor.

nominee (NOM-in-ee)–Person who has been considered for an award.

sophomore (SOF-a-more)–A student in a second year of high school or college.

INDEX